Wire

MW01268848

Making For Beginners

Made Simple

Complete Picture Step By Step Guide On How To Make Your Own Wire Wrapped Jewelry with Ease at the comfort of Your Home

Petrina Purser

TABLE OF CONTENTS

INTRODUCTION

Jewelry making is a particularly magnificent interest however it very well may be hard to tell where to begin! For novices it tends to be overpowering with regards to looking for adornments supplies, setting up a workbench and learning new procedures.

On the off chance that you have at any point contemplated figuring out how to enclose stones by wire to make adornments however didn't have the foggiest idea where to begin, you've gone to the perfect spot. Wire wrapping stones is in reality a lot simpler than it looks and figuring out how to do it empowers you to make excellent, stand-out adornments pieces utilizing a couple of essential materials. Truth be told, all you need to begin is a gemstone, some wire and two kinds of forceps. Continue to peruse to find how you can begin making extraordinary adornments by wire-wrapping precious stones.

As of late, be that as it may, gems spread the word about utilizing a method as wire wrapping has gotten very famous. As opposed to utilizing a setting, the gemstones utilized in wire-wrapped pieces are gotten set up utilizing slight wire. An incredible aspect concerning this procedure is that it's exceptionally easy to learn. It's additionally an entirely moderate alternative as it just requires a couple of cheap apparatuses and materials.

CHAPTER 1

MAKING A WEB WIRE WRAP

This web wrap is best for stones that are either genuinely level or have a slanted arch. Stones with high, level edges will be somewhat more baffling to work with. In any case, it's an incredible style taxis with slender edges, for sporadic shapes like ocean glass, or for dainty and level central pieces, similar to vintage catches.

It very well may be a decent easygoing wrap, you can make it more rural by purposefully making circles of various sizes and pulling them more tight, or you can dress it up by adding a globule dot to each circle for additional radiance.

WHAT YOU NEED

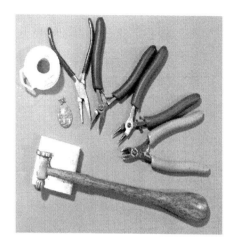

- cabochon

(20mm-40mm, domed round or oval is most effortless)

- 18-20 ga wire

- 28-24 ga wire

- wire cutters

- level nose pincers

- round nose pincers

- hammer and blacksmith's iron

Discretionary however accommodating:

- nylon nose pincers

- pen, weaving needle

- bail making pincers

- estimating tape

- creepy crawly dot

- pin

START WITH THE FRAME

Slice 18-20 ga wire to stone outline + 4". From the middle make a casing 1/8" to 1/4" more modest than the cabochon. (When utilizing a round cabochon a spool of string can be an extraordinary structure.)

When the edge is molded, twist the additional wire 90 degrees up from the edge. Sledge the edge tenderly to solidify it. (Try not to pound the two wires standing up, these will turn into your bail.)

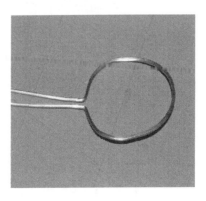

BAIL

Making a Bail* (*leave the Legs Up and Skip This Step If You Want to Make a Woven Bail)

1/4" up from crossroads, twist the long wires forward 1/4" and around your round nose forceps (or round object of the correct size) towards the back to make a bail. The tails should hang down.

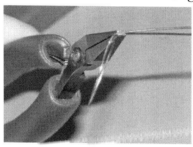

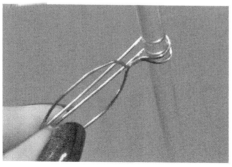

Fold over the stem with a 3-4" of wire. End with a twisting in front. Winding the two back wires to the casing. They'll help hold the stone in the back.

THE NETTING

Cut 1 ½ yards of fine wire. Fold one end over the casing 2 or multiple times just to one side of the bail.

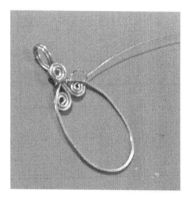

(It will slide around. Simply slip it back.)

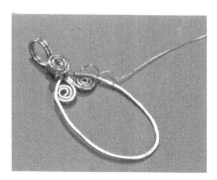

Make a circle with the little wire, calling attention to from the casing like a minuscule petal. Eye it, or use something tight and round to 'measure' circles.

COVERING THE LOOP

TO CLOSE THE LOOP, make a shut circle, string the wire under the edge and get it back up through the circle. Pull it tight, however not with the goal that it loses shape.

Rehash to make another circle of about a similar size. Proceed until circles are equally divided all around the edge.

SIZE CHECKING AND SECOND ROLLING

Spot the taxi on the edge. In the event that the circles don't show, wrap once about the bail base to wind up back toward the start.

Start a second external column by wrapping under the highest point of the main circle, at that point getting the wire up through the new circle. Pull adequately tight to remain without losing the new circle.

On the off chance that the circles show, start the following column against the stone, holding the taxi set up. Presently the movement will be over the wire and the down through the circle. Same join from an alternate point!

WRAPPING IT UP

After each circle, pull solidly. Hold the taxi with one hand while pulling so it gets caught as opposed to pushed. It will begin looking not so much daisy but rather more web.

Continue to circle around-if a few join end up too little avoid a circle to even them out. After 3-4 rounds test the stone. In the event that it feels tight, close off the net whenever. In the event that it shifts, proceed.

To end the net, wrap behind and around where the main circle of that keep going column got on the principal circle of the past line. Fold it over again and slice as near the 'hitch' as could be expected.

(Discretionary) Finish with an appeal or dab. Rather than cutting the wire, feed it through the globule and focus the dab over your 'hitch', at that point get where you completed your net again and cut the wire off.

Note: the number of columns it takes to get the stone has less to do with the size of the stone and more to do with the circle size and stone cut.

Bigger circles by and large methods less columns in some cases two will do. A stone with dainty edges climbing to a high arch will require less columns than a compliment stone or one with high sides.

WOVEN BALL

it's simpler to do this subsequent to catching the stone, so make web first and leave legs standing up. Add 5" to outline rather than 4" to give some space to breathe.

Twist the long wires to diagram a leaf shape around 1 ½ long. Wrap one finish of a yard of fine wire a few times around one of the upstanding legs to get it.

This wrap is figure 8s in wire. From the getting wraps, cross to the next thick wire, wrap under and around that wire 3x.

Cross back to the primary wire going over and around 3x. Rehash. More than one side, under the other.

Completing THE WOVEN

When the whole shape is wrapped, twist the woven bail forward then back around round nose pincers or round execute so the tails run down the rear of the stone.

Utilize the actually joined fine wire to 'line' around front of bail base. You can utilize it to add a dab before the bail, at that point cut.

Fold one back tail over multiple times. Bring the other around to front and polish off with a twisting.

CHAPTER 2

MAKING WIRE WRAPPED WRAP RING

This is a customary wire wrap ring - with a wind. In a real sense. The wonderful and durable band folds over your finger so you don't have to stress over ring estimating, making it ideal for blessing giving.

WHAT YOU NEED

Wire:

You can utilize any sort of nontoxic metal wire, however I like to by adornments grade wire on the web. Wire Sculpture and Rio Grande are amazing sources. In case you're simply starting I suggest copper or bronze. They're cheap and look incredible with clean or patina. To begin purchase in any event 5 feet of 22 measure, dead delicate, SQUARE wire and 2 feet of 21 or 22 check, dead delicate, HALF ROUND wire.

Apparatuses:

Apparatuses are vital. I utilized modest gems forceps (~$10) for some time, however once I was certain I would remain with wire wrapping, I got great ones (~$50) It had an immense effect, particularly in how tired my hands would get. On the off chance that you do this, hold tight to your modest instruments - there's consistently a utilization pincers you will not stress over. The essential apparatuses you should begin are:

Level nose forceps

Round nose forceps

Wire cutters

Marker

Ring mandrel

Ruler

Discretionary:

Globules or gems that fit on the wire. 4mm and up is typically acceptable.

WIRE CUTTING

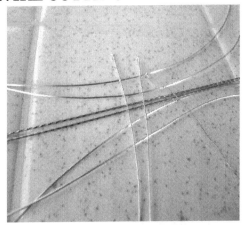

Measure

Recall that this ring is customizable, so don't stress excessively if your estimations appear to be somewhat off anytime. That being said, here are the estimation guidelines:

Take a piece of string and fold it over your finger or ring mandrel (on the off chance that you know your size). Go once around and afterward some other time most of the way around with each side of the string. At that point add 3 extra inches. Utilizing a ruler, measure what you just separated on your string. This will be the length of one strand wire. You'll cut all square wire strands against this length.

My length ended up being 8 inches. It is smarter to decide in favor cutting too long then not having sufficient wire when you wrap. This will be the length of the 22 check, square, dead delicate wire. Cut six strands of this length. I cut 4 of silver and 2 of copper to make it simpler to see the distinction in the strands and what's going on with the undertaking. You can configuration any example you like from any wire.

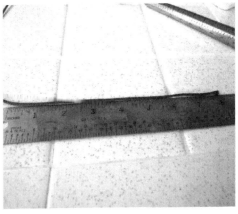

Presently cut five half round bits of wire. Make them one and a half inches each.

On the off chance that you need to wind any of the wire, this is the ideal opportunity. This makes a decent improving component to your plan. I turned the two place copper wires.

Making A BUNDLE

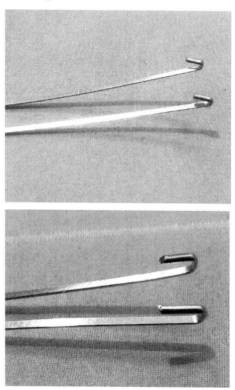

The six wires are wrapped along with the half round wire into a pack. The group is the base for the ring band. The article is to make a level strip held together at five focuses. The short bits of 1/2 round wire will hold the square wires together.

To Start:

Get one piece of 1/2 round wire and utilize the level nose pincers to twist 3-4 mm of the top over. At that point the twist marginally. Ensure the level side of the wire is within surface. This will fit perfectly around the square wire. Rehash with every one of the short half round pieces.

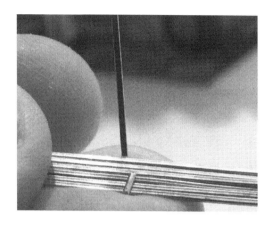

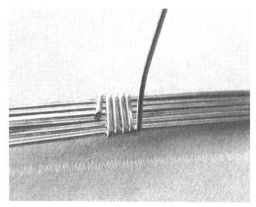

Next hold the square wires together next to each other. You may have to squirm them around a little to get them to arrange. At that point snare the twist of the 1/2 round wire more than one edge as appeared.

Give a delicate crush with the level nose pincers to get. (When wrapping, the front of the wraps ought to be 90 degrees to the group wires. The rear of the wraps are generally calculated.) Now hold the square wire pack with the level nose forceps extremely near where you will fold the short pieces over. Begin winding the 1/2 round wire around the group, however stop each time you make a turn and give the wires a delicate press with the level nose pincers. Hope to be moving the pack and the pincers around a ton, changing hands when you need to.

Wrap the 1/2 round wire around the group this way 3-4 times and end on the rear of the pack. Cut the abundance 1/2 round wire with the goal that it covers the back 3 – 4mm.

THE RING BUNDLE

Beginning with the center wrap and working outward, make five complete wraps (reasonably equally divided), over around 3 inches.

MOLDING THE BAND

At the point when you have a decent group with five wraps you can begin molding the ring.

Hold the group on the ring mandrel with your thumb over the focal wrap. At that point delicately begin bowing the sides

once again the ring mandrel. Return
around the and up to the opposite side.

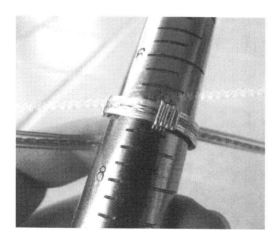

KEEP SHAPING

There ought to be a solitary band in the rear of the ring and covering groups in front.

FANNING OUT THE WIRES

like to tenderly fan out the wires to see precisely what I need to work with.

MAKING FILIGREE

Presently it's an ideal opportunity to add embellishments and finish the closures. You can utilize the accompanying ideas or utilize your own #1 wire procedures.

Here's the place where the genuine creativity comes in. The filigree is the sensitive looking whirls and dips that make up the plan of the wire wrap. You make it with the last details of wire after the band is the correct size and shape. Precisely what you do is up to you, however make sure to add your dots while the wire is still genuinely straight.

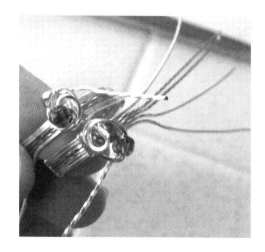

BEING ARTISTIC WITH SOME DECORATIVE TECHNIQUES

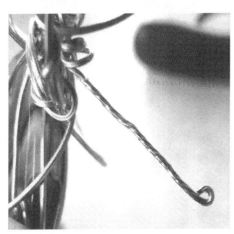

Rosettes

This is likely the most well-known plan component in wire wrapping. You make a rosette by utilizing your round nose forceps to make a little round circle toward the finish of a wire. At that point wind the circle into a tight twisting utilizing level nosed forceps. To do this hold the wire in one hand and pivot the wires in the other hand a quarter turn at a time. You can make the rosettes with contorted or untwisted wire for various looks.

Circles

Making circles and shapes with the wire is loads of fun, yet don't go too enormous or the wire will twist too without any problem. Continue diving wires tight to the setting and figure out how to get the end on another wire.

Wind

Utilize level nosed pincers to hold a free wire end and curve.

NOTE

In case you don't know what to do, add a couple of gems (1 each) to a few wires and slice all the wire finishes to around a 1/2 inch. At that point make rosettes out of the multitude of closures.

COMPLETED WORK

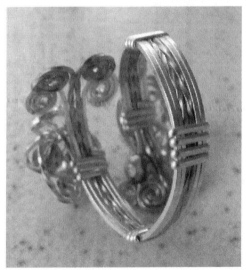

At the point when you're finished with embellishing components, trim off any additional wire (you can save it for different activities) and fold any last details under. Feel the ring with your fingers for harsh spots and afterward rub the front and back on a piece of texture. In the event that you track down any sharp spots or wires that get; document, trim or wrap up the issue wires until everything is totally smooth. On the off chance that anytime your ring gets distorted, just set it back on the ring mandrel and press it back into shape. On the off chance that it's difficult to shape with you fingers, utilize a nylon or rawhide hammer.

Presently you can add a patina, buff or potentially seal your ring on the off chance that you need.

THE END

Made in United States
Troutdale, OR
12/29/2023

16539552R00029